W9-AGB-314

THE
DIGESTIVE
SYSTEM

BY SUSAN H. GRAY

Published by The Child's World®
1980 Lookout Drive • Mankato, MN 56003-1705
800-599-READ • www.childsworld.com

Acknowledgments
The Child's World®: Mary Berendes, Publishing Director
Red Line Editorial: Editorial direction
The Design Lab: Design
Amnet: Production

Content Consultant: R. John Solaro, Ph.D., Distinguished
University Professor and Head, Department of Physiology and
Biophysics, University of Illinois Chicago

Photographs ©: Sebastian Kaulitzki/Shutterstock Images, cover
(background), 1 (background), 19; Shutterstock Images, cover
(foreground), 1 (foreground); Big Cheese Photo/Thinkstock, 4;
Leonello Calvetti/Shutterstock Images, 7; Monkey Business
Images/Shutterstock Images, 8, 12; Deyan Georgiev/
Shutterstock Images, 11; iStockphoto/Thinkstock, 14; Jane
September/Shutterstock Images, 16; Diana Taliun/Shutterstock
Images, 20

ISBN 9781626873353
LCCN 2014930672

Printed in the United States of America
Mankato, MN
July, 2014
PA02221

ABOUT THE AUTHOR

Susan H. Gray has a bachelor's and a master's degree in zoology. In her 25 years as an author, she has written many medical articles, grant proposals, and children's books. Ms. Gray and her husband, Michael, live in Cabot, Arkansas.

TABLE OF CONTENTS

CHAPTER 1

Never Again

Tony and his friends were eating lunch together under an oak tree. Today was the class picnic. The food was great. Tony had two hot dogs and a pile of potato chips. He drank three glasses of lemonade.

When you eat, your digestive system works hard to break down all of the food.

Tony was stuffed! The picnic was not over yet. His teacher brought out a plate of cupcakes.

Tony groaned. He loved cupcakes. But he could not eat another thing. He leaned back against the tree and closed his eyes.

He slid his hand over his stomach. It felt round and tight. His stomach had stretched as far as it could. It was working hard to deal with the food Tony had eaten. Special fluids were coming from his stomach's walls. The fluids were mixing with the hot dogs and buns. They were blending in with the potato chips. The fluids began slowly breaking everything down.

Tony did not care what happened in his stomach. He knew he had eaten way too much. He groaned a second time and sighed, "I'll never do that again."

CHAPTER 2

What Is the Digestive System?

To digest something means to break it down and **absorb** it. The digestive system is the group of organs that breaks down and absorbs food.

The main organs of this system are hollow and joined end-to-end. They look like a tube. The mouth is the first part of the digestive system. Next comes the esophagus. This leads to the stomach. The intestines make up the last part of this system.

Two other organs are also involved in digestion. These are the liver and pancreas. They are not part of the tube but are nearby. They make the juices that help digest food.

One job of the digestive system is to change food into materials the body can use. The body cannot use most foods as they are. The foods are made of **molecules**. The molecules are too large to be useful to the body.

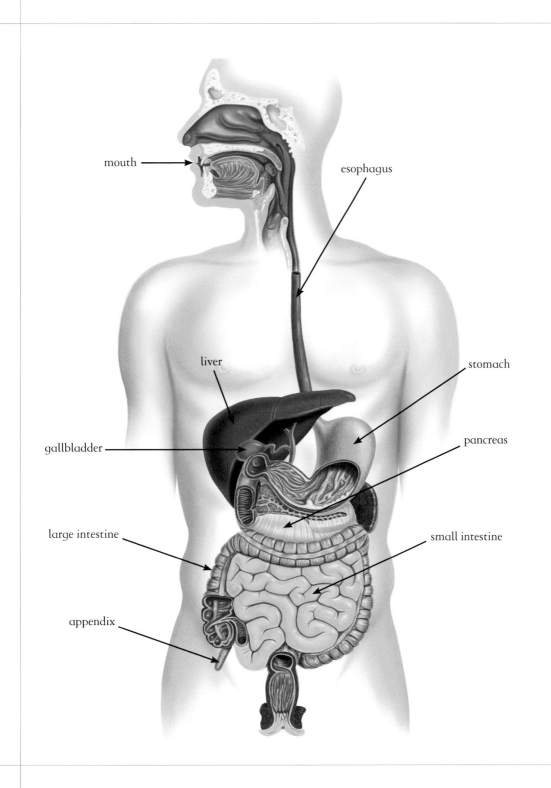

mouth

esophagus

liver

stomach

gallbladder

pancreas

large intestine

small intestine

appendix

There are many parts that make up the digestive system. Each part has an important job.

The digestive system breaks the molecules down. The body uses these **nutrients** for all of its normal activities.

Your blood moves nutrients through your body.
This gives you the energy to play.

Another job of the digestive system is to get nutrients into the bloodstream. Then the blood carries them through the body. The nutrients travel to places where the body can use them.

The inside of the digestive system is wet and slippery. This is because of the many glands lining it. Digestive glands are little bundles of cells that produce fluids. Some glands of the digestive system produce fluids that keep the food moist. Some produce liquids that help break down the food.

The walls of the digestive tube have blood vessels and nerves. They also have muscles. The muscles squeeze and relax, making the digestive organs move. Normally, you cannot feel your stomach or intestines move. But sometimes you can hear sounds coming from them. They are quite busy, especially after a meal. Their movements push food through the tube.

CHAPTER 3

What Happens in the Mouth?

The digestive system starts with the mouth. This is where food first comes into the body. Teeth bite off pieces of food. The teeth in the front of the mouth are sharp. They are made for biting and tearing food. The teeth in the back of the mouth are wide. These teeth are made for chewing. They grind food into smaller pieces. The tongue moves the food around. This helps the teeth chew everything. Little bumps on the tongue are lined with taste buds. These detect the different flavors of food as it is being chewed.

Salivary glands go to work before food enters

DID YOU KNOW?
Bumps on the tongue come in several different shapes. You will see some large, round bumps at the very back of your tongue.

Most of the tiny bumps on your tongue help you taste your food.

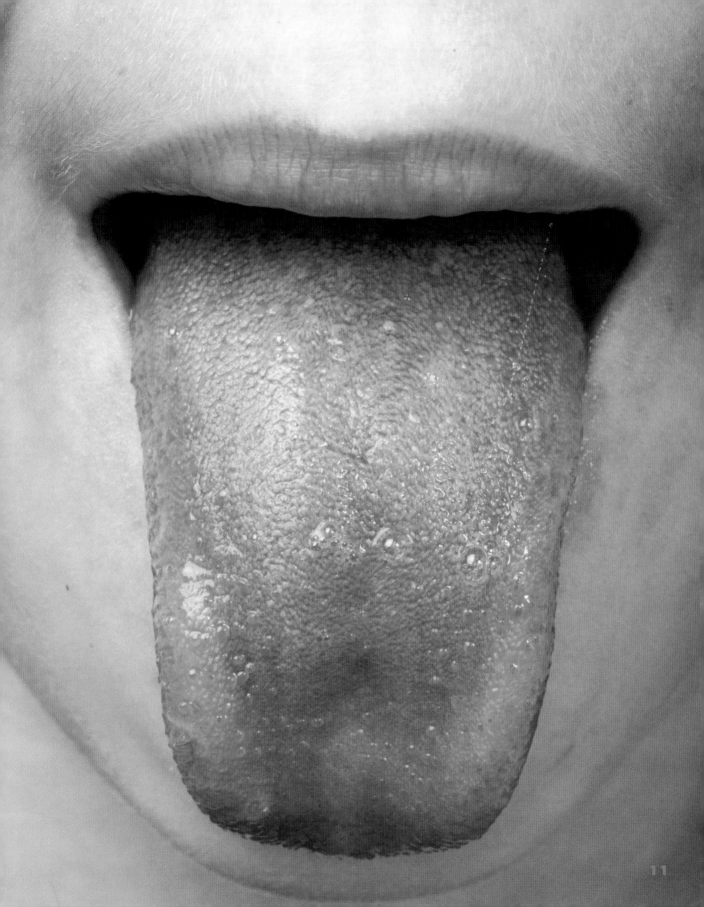

11

the mouth. These glands make saliva, or spit. Three pairs of glands release saliva into the mouth. The first pair is in the cheeks. These glands are on either side of the mouth in front of the ears.

The other two saliva gland pairs lie within the lower jaw. Little tubes run from the glands and open into the mouth. Saliva from the glands makes the food moist. It also starts breaking down some foods into smaller molecules. When a person is nervous,

Your mouth is the beginning of the digestive system.
It starts to break food down into smaller pieces.

chemicals are released to stop the flow of saliva. That makes the mouth feel dry.

Once food is ground up, the tongue shoves it to the back of the mouth. Muscles in this area squeeze together. They push food into the throat. As food starts down the throat, a little flap called the epiglottis acts. It flops over and covers the opening of the windpipe. This keeps food from going into the lungs.

Food moves down the esophagus. This tube runs from the back of the mouth down to the stomach. Glands in the esophagus walls add fluid as the food moves by. Food does not fall to the stomach by gravity. The esophagus has muscular walls. These muscles gently squeeze and relax, moving food to the stomach.

CHAPTER 4

What Happens in the Stomach?

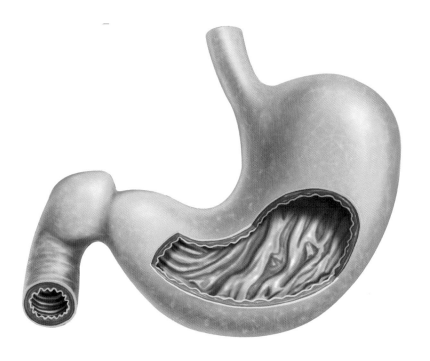

The stomach is hollow and shaped like the letter *J*. The stomach walls are made of muscle tissue. The muscles relax when food enters. This lets the stomach stretch out to hold that food.

The stomach is moist and wrinkled inside.

Cells in the stomach wall make fluids that mix with the food. Some cells let out fluids that break down meat. Other cells let out fluids that break down **fats**. Some cells produce a strong acid. Other cells produce mucus. Mucus coats the inside of the stomach. It protects the stomach lining from the acid.

After food comes in, the stomach goes to work. The muscular walls squeeze and relax. This pushes the food around. The cells release their fluids. Food becomes covered with acid and mucus. It mixes with fluids that break it down into smaller molecules. When the stomach is done, food is wet and mushy. This mushy material is called chyme.

CHAPTER 5

What Happens in the Small Intestine?

Chyme moves out of the stomach and into the small intestine. This tube is about 20 feet (6.1 meters) long in an adult. Three other important organs are near the small intestine. These are the

Food is still traveling through your small intestine a few hours after you eat.

pancreas, the liver, and the gallbladder. Tubes run from these organs into the small intestine. Fluids go through the tubes and mix with food in the intestine.

Fluid from the pancreas breaks down **proteins**, fats, and **carbohydrates**. It also weakens the strong acid from the stomach. Fluid from the liver goes into the gallbladder. Then it goes into the small intestine. This fluid is called bile. It helps the small intestine work on fats.

The small intestine breaks down most food. Then the body can absorb the nutrients. The nutrients soak into the intestine's walls. Tiny blood vessels in the walls pick up these nutrients. The nutrients enter the blood and are sent throughout the body.

Food takes hours to move through the small intestine. Muscles in the intestine walls squeeze and relax. This slowly propels food forward.

CHAPTER 6

What About the Large Intestine?

Food reaches the end of the small intestine after several hours. Most proteins, fats, and carbohydrates have been broken down. They have moved into the bloodstream. The leftover food moves into the large intestine.

The large intestine is shorter than the small intestine. It is about 5 feet (1.5 meters) long in an adult. The large intestine starts on the right side of the body. It runs straight up and across to the left side. Then it runs back down and out of the body.

DID YOU KNOW?
Greasy and fatty foods are harder for your digestive system to handle. These foods take longer to digest.

The large intestine also has muscular walls. As the walls move, they push the leftover food forward

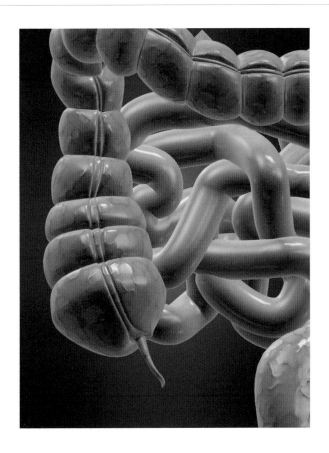

and sometimes backward. As the food is pushed, water and salts are removed. These are drawn into the blood. The remaining food leaves the body as waste.

The appendix is attached to the large intestine. No one knows exactly what it does. Sometimes it becomes diseased. This may happen when the digestive system is infected. A doctor must remove the diseased appendix. Otherwise, it may cause more trouble.

The appendix is attached to the large intestine.

CHAPTER 7

Why Do You Get an Upset Stomach?

Sometimes bacteria or viruses in the digestive system cause sickness. These germs can give a person an upset stomach. Or they may make the intestines hurt. The germs may even cause a queasy feeling. This feeling

Amusement park rides can also cause motion sickness for some people.

may make a person throw up. The body usually gets over the germs in one or two days.

Motion sickness can also disturb the digestive system. This sometimes happens when people are in cars, on boats, or on planes. Germs do not cause this. It happens when the brain cannot sort out all of the different signals coming to it. The brain cannot make sense of them. When the brain gets confused, a person begins to feel dizzy. The stomach may tighten up. The person may even sweat and throw up.

The digestive system usually does not have such problems. It works day and night. It breaks down the food we eat and moves it. The digestive system takes care of big meals when we overeat. It handles little snacks. The digestive system prepares food to be used by every cell in the body.

GLOSSARY

absorb (ab-ZORB) To absorb something is to soak it up. The digestive system is a group of organs that absorbs food.

carbohydrates (KAR-bo-HY-drates) Carbohydrates are materials found in sugary or starchy foods. Fluids from the pancreas break down carbohydrates.

fats (FATZ) Fats are materials found in oily or greasy foods. Some fluids in the body break down fats.

molecules (MOL-uh-kyoolz) Molecules are extremely small parts of something. Food is made of molecules.

nutrients (NOO-tree-uhnts) Nutrients are the things found in foods needed for life and health. The body needs nutrients for energy.

proteins (PROH-teenz) Proteins are materials found in meat, fish, eggs, dairy products, and some other foods. Fluid from the pancreas breaks down proteins.

LEARN MORE

BOOKS

Gardner, Jane P. *Take a Closer Look at Your Stomach.*
Mankato, MN: The Child's World, 2014.

Manolis, Kay. *The Digestive System.*
Minneapolis: Bellwether Media, 2009.

VanVoorst, Jenny Fretland. *Take a Closer Look at Your
Teeth*. Mankato, MN: The Child's World, 2014.

WEB SITES

Visit our Web site for links about the digestive system:
childsworld.com/links

Note to Parents, Teachers, and Librarians: We routinely
verify our Web links to make sure they are safe and active
sites. So encourage your readers to check them out!

INDEX